After the Creek

poems by

Autumn McClintock

Finishing Line Press
Georgetown, Kentucky

After the Creek

ACKNOWLEDGMENTS

Warm thanks to the editors of the following magazines where these poems first
appeared:

Apiary: How to Communicate
B O D Y: Finale
The Carolina Quarterly: Cable Car/Clouds
The Citron Review: Celebration
The Collagist: Great Pacific Garbage Patch
elimae: News
Green Mountains Review: Annunciation
Juked: Approach
Pembroke Magazine: Dinnertime
Redivider: Obstinance
RHINO: The Herd
Stoneboat Literary Journal: The Trees
THRUSH: Madrid, NM

Publisher: Leah Maines

Editor: Christen Kincaid

Cover Art: Karl Pilato, www.karlpilato.com

Author Photo: Naisha Patterson

Cover Design: Elizabeth Maines

Printed in the USA on acid-free paper.
Order online: www.finishinglinepress.com
          also available on amazon.com

Author inquiries and mail orders:
Finishing Line Press
P. O. Box 1626
Georgetown, Kentucky 40324
U. S. A.

Table of Contents

1.

HOW TO COMMUNICATE

Find a marker—brown, blue, or green. Uncap it.

Make a fist with your non-writing hand, thumb on the inside. You're not hitting anyone.

Rest the fisted hand on the table, on the fleshy side-pad where the ulna meets the lunate carpal bone. Your tucked thumb's knuckle faces up at you.

Using the marker, draw two dots, 1/2 inch apart, on the rise of your index finger's knuckle. The dots should be friendly.

Pull the thumb down but don't release it from the fist. Do this several times. Look at the oddly shaped hole you've created: this is the mouth. And the dots the marker made: these are the eyes.

Tell your hand's face what you've been thinking today. Tell it how you banged your hip on the corner of the desk and made a bruise. Or how your neck's kinked from sleeping in the wrong pose too long. Tell it why you chew your nails.

Now hunker down, your ear near to the mouth. Let the thumb do its wagging. Hear what your hand's mouth says to you, and feel its eyes on your hairline. Whatever you have to say to yourself, say it this way.

NEWS

Made to recognize evil.
You are made to.

I want a go at the nose, teeth,
line moving across the page; you will understand it.

You will take up the body,
justified unburied.
Your father or dictator,
past human, a pile of skin.

Get in there with the best adjective.
Language our way around it.

THE TREES

No one comes with the saw.
Branches have their way
in the wind, poke

a hole in the glass,
crack in thunder and dangle
over the shuddering grass.

Whistle of the axe
nowhere near, no divot
or warning of the push.

You are a forest now,
tangled beyond untangling,
grown blind with moss

and mushroom.
Reach out your hands
into the dark.

A different kind of silence
with reason to be afraid.

DINNERTIME

A bowl passed, bread torn,
talk of a science experiment

or history lesson. Once divided
the French repaired by revolution.

One with authority demands
the drinking of milk.

One slips chewed broccoli into a napkin
or to the dog, if it is alive

and not making itself to bone in the yard.
On vacation can we ride the rollercoaster,

one asks, but the others feel a tingle of fear.
Fork rasps a plate.

The smallest wonders what it's like
to go fast as possible and upside-down.

BIRTHDAY

Slab of carrot cake in cellophane.
No candle, no ache for doll or bike.

Aching comes now
in the calves

where running's protested,
shins are suddenly known.

My father describes the evening
I was born, blaze of leaf

in sun. This singular event
not my memory

or owned experience,
and he, the one creator left.

It and I are his alone.

RESISTANCE

It may not be anywhere

you've heard of.

Cloud or cliff or field.

Hang onto this

wine poured

in the wrong kind of cup,

leaves a ring

on the blond bench.

Through it, the lowing

light slips, hits

the ground worn bald from shuffling:

tap, scuffle, maybe, thirst.

SELF PORTRAIT IN BLUE

Heat from the metal grate

up in waves.

Beyond, the Cira Center

gives the finger or a blade's edge.

I make you my business.

Cross-legged,

place where a child could be.

The cancer I'll create of unused cells

long waiting in chest or ovaries,

then flung

as trash in a car wreck.

I bet we're the same as everyone in this bar.

THE ODDS

I want to up the ante, stack large
the table before betting begins, to stretch

diagonal across this room so my shoulders pop.
No nightlight but the lighted night

upon the drive, crickets, ears
swallowed with pulse and screech.

Also want wine in a plastic cup and a rack
of pool-balls in no good order. Then red hot

salsa, like cherry-of-your-cigarette hot.
A new need, leaning so you crave the bridge,

behind the back, however you make it. Break.
Sweat-heavy palms, crush,

voice like a Lincoln hitting
deep down the spine. I want you

to strum, "get all the news I need on the weather report"
Dat n-dah, dat n-dah. I want scratch.

Mosquitoes to bite and tell me here I am.

CELEBRATION

Rain soaks, hangs low the branches—
leaves wet as the first time.

Three-legged dog takes it slow, knows
there's no other getting there.

It wasn't too cold or too warm
far east as we would go, admitting

we could not add a single hour.
Now I say to you, passing the bedroom door

this new evening,
even your shadow I love.

AFTER THE CREEK / DRIED FLOWER

What looks like a spider is a flower
pressed flat. Given, then tucked away.
Petal-shrunken legs
crook'd in all directions.

Funny, you handing it as a lover,
eyelash flutter. On a large rock
in the creek I turned it sweet,
folding into a book.

Boulders came here by ice age,
slow crack and thaw,
delivering us a place
for slant of sun and climb.

A boy baits a hook, stands
shin-deep, ignoring all but the line,
to find what moves or seems to,
the rushing underneath.

LESSON ON PRAYER

Dear Lord, it should start and end,
not my will but yours be done. These days
mine go, (*supplication*) pretend

it isn't I, Dear Lord, long ago spit out
as John said in Revelation
for being tepid as a carpet, bland as a knee,

lukewarm. Go wild (*thanksgiving*)
for farro with basil, iced tea,
the cool end of summer, curve

around the bend, for track and train,
pool in morning light, swing set
(*adoration*) in morning light, dome

of the Orthodox church, amen,
and (*confession*) forgive me, you might say.

2.

APPROACH

By the time you've read this, I will be leader
of the marching band: *hup-two-three,*

76 Al-Samoud missiles eat the big parade.
Choosing music for this anniversary,

we build a building to end all buildings. My pride could
beat up your pride. My plane is full of tinny-tin-tin.

Let's re-watch the billow of smoke.
Captain Anonymous circles the house

looking to mustachio our face.
Through all devices and devising we have come to:

high fructose corn syrup. The Red Sea
full up with Coke cans. Coke cans, full up with burqas.

When they ask us what it's like to be American,
we say, it's like when the scientists decided

Pluto wasn't a planet anymore because he knew,
but he was the only one who knew.

Thank you Lawrence Welk. We will never forget
your accordion and pretty dancing girls. Thank you

pretty dancing girls.

THE DEAD MAN

Even your hair a paler gray,

skin like I would imagine.

It is the first time I have touched one,

and one is you, my own blood

pooling at the lowest point of gravity—

your back and useless legs.

There are many ways to remember,

and this is one.

Blue light, blue cheek.

Clutch whoever is here, standing.

Clutch at the shadow

from the bathroom door, ajar.

OBSTINANCE

Tight hanging to this cliff
blue brick 500 years.

I am the very pebbles
a shore too stark to lie on.

You are dying, of course
it was true,

but only like the rest.
The clock

a crumbling *pensione*
with cheap best wine,

pale sheets.
Do not be ashamed

letting go the coast
shale by shale.

If there is a boat,
husks crunched in the hull,

nets stinking of brine,
let it come.

ANNUNCIATION

Learning Jesus incarnates
the moment the angel appears
to the Virgin girl, Mary, merely

betrothed to Joseph and knowing
not him or any other man.
Remembering [insignificant

name for vastness] fields
crossing Illinois, Iowa whose union
with their place grows essential, awful.

What's red to us, blue when our waving
bodies by bodies, these green rows
rising as luminous teeth,

saying *take, eat, do this.*
Beautiful spacious majestic crowned:
grain and savior, your end so foretold.

MADRID, NM

Kick aside the other bones.
Whatever body it may be,
bury it.

Dirt and crag,
the desert will drain
like a common sink.

Lick the sand
deep caught in teeth
to see if it flavors
or gives way.

All horizons chocked with scrub,
dotted between with snow.

Road hewn through
as wagon went,
crossed by fawn and steer.

Center strewn and bloodied
from the red, strange earth,
we kneel.

FROM CHIMNEY ROCK

Outlook above the river,
a canoe with just one rower,

tent way back
from the rocky beach.

Nostalgias carom
this place, knock one another

like the children, legs hanging over
their black "O"s.

They bob and shiver,
woosh forward and bounce, a shriek

rises up, and she's nearly certain
the shriek is joy.

CABLE CAR / CLOUDS

What I'll call a falcon banks
across and the sun is huge
the clouds close clouds
my soon to be friends
it's handshaking and nodding
and I am very well liked
so far for my generous
eye contact and we trade
about kids jobs
and I become very interested
in cloud work Stratus
who's here with his friends
who seems like a downer
but instead makes brilliant
the greens who is developing a project
with Lenticular in a couple hours
or a day we will be drenched
in their good work and run off
under the eaves of the snack shop
and pack into the van
and drive away but until then
I'll rock back down
the mountain in an ecstasy
rocking and nodding
and descending
wrapped in the world.

FINALE

He has gone to find what God there is.
Tracks and their hollows filled with stone.

It is not the lamppost but the leaves,
throwing light over muddled parks and cars.

Someone practices violin—
between us a stucco wall.

After this block, I won't come to the end
but will stop where the key fits the lock,

the strong box: a strapped sheath of letters,
a woolen cap and whatever I didn't ill spend.

Let us give thanks.
We danced,

though promised to others,
we could not help dancing.

GREAT PACIFIC GARBAGE PATCH

when you die and I am still young
I'll go out on some raft

all the birds we've studied
have plastic in them 100%

those whale lovers
become drastic

one who scrapes the ocean
they make shampoo bottles

from reclaimed bits
one scientist pleads

let's work with what's already on the planet
we are on the goddamn planet

when you are dead
i'll remember styrofoam

we failed to cradle
like this gull like

no child ever

BACKYARD

Makeshift laundry line strung taut
but in the since-years sagged.
Each pin wooden to gray, metal hinge
a twirl of rust. To hang clothes dry
one must practice the want of stiffness.

We rue the mustard greens,
inedible now the cats have come,
but gone to seed, they sprout
a turgid stalk topped yellow with buds.
There, the butterfly clusters,

and we are glad not to eat, to go on
in the nearly-summer sun,
skin turned an illicit pink. Oh butterfly,
you are white and white
forever against the lettuce leaf and soil.

THE HERD

Suddenly snowy, cars
brake-lighting all the way to New Holland.

After Thanksgiving they're heavier
on the pedal with a gut-full.

One skids, then another
into the oncoming lane.

One won't turn off its blinker.
Left. Left. Lef—

We ease past a cop car
who got done wailing

at the scene.
Then I see them

behind the fence, somehow out in this,
black and white as an old photo

even through the sleet,
each head hung like a hand

fallen from a lap.

Autumn McClintock lives in Philadelphia, works at the public library, and serves on the City's Poet Laureate Selection Committee. She holds an MFA in Creative Writing from Emerson College. Poems of hers have recently appeared in *B O D Y*, *The Carolina Quarterly*, *The Citron Review*, *The Collagist*, *Drunken Boat*, *Green Mountains Review*, *LEVELER*, *Redivider*, *RHINO*, *THRUSH*, *Weave Magazine*, and others. Her essay, "Responsible for Death," appears in the 2013 anthology *The Poet's Sourcebook*, published by Autumn House Press (no relation). She is a staff reader for *Ploughshares*. An avid sewer and baseball fan, she lives with her husband, the poet Craig Giandomenico, in a tiny row home.

www.ingramcontent.com/pod-product-compliance
Lightning Source LLC
LaVergne TN
LVHW041329080426
835513LV00008B/655